TRAGEDY TO TRIUMPH

FORGIVENESS IS THE KEY

Cheryl A. Miller

DEDICATION

To my Lord and Savior, Jesus Christ, and to
the glory of God the Father

ACKNOWLEDGMENTS

To my wonderful husband, Jerry, who has been such an encourager and without whom, this book would not have been written.

To our son, Scott, who stepped forward and took charge when we could not; who quietly, without praise or glory, has been a solid rock and a marvelous example of a great work ethic.

To our son, Michael, who at a very young age was my little prayer partner and went along with me to every speaking engagement and conference, and was by my side through the development of Agape' as a year round program, yet never complained.

To our daughter, Dawn, who partnered with me in developing the first stages of Agape, who was a loving daughter and who now lives with the Lord for eternity.

To Nancy and Ed Fitzgerald and their loving family, who took care of Michael while I was recovering in the hospital after being shot, and then took care of me when I was released.

To the many people who have served on the Agape' Board of Directors over the years and to the hundreds of volunteers, who have given thousands of hours of service to Agape.

To the donors, who have given money, materials, and services to Agape'.

To the Agape staff, past and present, who have faithfully demonstrated God's unconditional agape' love to everyone who has entered this very special place.

And of course to God's very special creature, the horse, who inspires and motivates each individual to reach his God given potential with unbridled hope.

TABLE OF CONTENTS

1.

TRAGEDY STRIKES

The bullet pierced my side, going through me like a burning sword, then exiting by my spine. I dropped to the floor of my living room with the gun now pointed at my head. Awaiting the final explosion into my skull, I looked into the eyes of my assailant and I spoke, "Bill, God loves you and I forgive you. Please don't do any more." Bill responded, "I don't care about your God. I don't care about your Jesus. I want you to suffer." The gun fired again. The stinging burn of the bullet hit my head.

It is said that at the moment of death your entire life flashes before you.

I was born in Austin, Texas. My dad was stationed there during World War II. Even though we moved back to Indianapolis before I was two years old, I considered myself a true blue Texas cowgirl. Of course that meant that I needed a horse. The problem with that was that we lived on the near east side of Indianapolis in front of my family's wholesale bakery. No room for a horse there.

My grandparents lived in the suburbs of Indy, so I thought for certain that I could have a pony stay in part of my grandpa's dog kennels where he raised champion beagles, but the answer was, "No." A pony was too big to stay in a dog kennel.

As a six year old, one of my favorite activities at grandma and grandpa's house was to look for pretty jewels and fossils in their stone driveway. As I searched the landscape, I talked to my very best friend, GOD. He knew how badly I wanted a pony, because I asked for one every night in my prayers. But this day, I had a different request. "God, I know that I can't have a pony right now because we don't have a place to keep one, but could I just have one for a day?" Moments later, CLIP CLOP! CLIP CLOP! There came a black and white spotted pony trotting down the middle of the street. No one was with it. The pony turned into my grandparents yard and began munching grass. I darted into the house, talking so fast that my grandma wasn't certain what she was hearing. "A what in the front yard? A PONY!"

After attaching a rope to its halter, we tied the pony to a tree. Grandma gave me her old brush and comb. I brushed the pony, combed its mane and tail, and got to ride it bareback with grandpa leading. I had a pony all day long, but now the sun was beginning to set. An unfamiliar car pulled into the driveway and out jumped a boy and girl from the back seat. They were shouting with excitement, "We found him. We found him. We found Spot." The children lived about a half a mile away on several acres. They had just gotten Spot, the pony, a few days before. Someone left Spot's gate unlocked that day and Spot decided to take a little trip. But I really knew what happened. God heard the prayer of a little six year old girl and gave me a pony for the day. I knew without a doubt that God was real and He hears us and answers us. His answer may be, "Yes." It may be, "No," or it may be, "Wait," but he always answers if we are truly listening.

2.

LOVE

God has always been very real to me and I loved everything in nature. I really loved going to my grandparent's summer home on a lake. The sounds of the water, the breeze from the lake, all of it was perfect. I was now fourteen years old. My younger brother, Steve, had invited a boy and girl from another cottage on the island to come to our house. The girl was my brother's age and the boy was sixteen, almost two years older than I was. Just as they arrived I discovered a baby bird that had fallen out of a nest in the large oak tree that shaded my grandparent's front yard. Jerry, the athletic sixteen year old, came to the baby bird's rescue by gently cradling the bird in one hand and courageously climbing the tree to place the fledgling back in its nest. If there is love at first sight, then I experienced it. Right then, that very moment, I knew that I was in love and that some day Jerry and

I would marry. Little did I know until much later that Jerry felt the same way about me.

My parents did not allow me to date - not until I turned fifteen, but they allowed me to enjoy the summer fun at the lake with other kids, including Jerry. Playing Monopoly in the screened in porch in the evenings, and volleyball, water tag, and boating during the days were all such fun, but then the summer was over. Time to return to Indianapolis and back to my sophomore year of high school. Would I see Jerry again? I would turn fifteen in the fall. Would we date? Would Jerry even call me now that summer was over?

Surprise! Jerry lived in Indianapolis, too. He attended a different high school, but lived only five miles away. Jerry was a year ahead of me in school. How quickly those years flew by, but then graduation came for Jerry and off he went to college. Would I loose my best friend? Would absence fade our relationship or make it even stronger?

Jerry came home almost every weekend to see me. Our plan was that as soon as I graduated from high school, we would ask my parents if we could get married. The time came. I loved my parents and I was very close to them. They thought I was very wise for my age, but I think that is because I always agreed with them. Something unusual happened the evening that we sat down to ask if we could get married. At that moment they no longer valued my wisdom. Dad's face turned red and his voice got shaky, mom began to sob, and pretty soon my dad and I were crying, too. Jerry looked very bewildered at what he was observing. How could one simple question bring about such emotion. Needless to say the answer was, "NO." But through sobs, they did say we would talk about it after I completed my first year of college. By the way, I was not allowed to go to the same college as Jerry.

3.

MARRIAGE

I graduated from high school and considered going out of state to a private all girl college in the South, but the distance would be too far away from Jerry. His college was just an hour south of Indianapolis, so I decided to go to Indiana University, just two hours south of Indy. We never missed a weekend without seeing each other and often talked during the week by phone. Christmas break arrived. I was now half way through my freshman year. We decided to sit down with my parents and ask again if we could get married. We thought that as soon as school was out for the summer, I would have finished one year of college and Jerry would be finished with two years of college. They wouldn't say NO now, would they? Unfortunately, they did say NO. They strongly suggested (but with no tears this time) that we wait until I completed my sophomore year.

We felt betrayed. We had thought that when my parents said to wait until I completed my Freshman year and we would talk about it, that they meant they would say YES. As spring began to end and the end of my freshman year was concluding, Jerry and I decided to elope. The problem that we immediately discovered after a little research was that in Indiana, a girl needed to be eighteen to marry, but a boy needed to be twenty-one. I was eighteen, so no problem, but Jerry was just twenty. After a little more research (you learn to do that in college) we decided that we would go across the state border to Michigan. There both the boy and the girl were of legal age to marry at age eighteen.

Early on Saturday, May 7, 1963, Jerry arrived at my dormitory. I was ready, so off we went to New Buffalo, Michigan. When we arrived at the Justice of the Peace's office, he told us that we needed to get our blood tests and apply for our license. We completed his assignments and returned back to Indiana and to my dorm that evening. Our plans were that the next week, on Saturday, May 11, that we would drive back to Michigan to be married.

I was really excited and looking forward to our life together, but this was the biggest decision of my life and my parents didn't even know. May 11, arrived. Off we went to Michigan. We had our gold wedding bands and I was wearing a new white sundress. I was silent on the three hour drive. Jerry asked me several times if I was all right. Each time I nodded my head yes without speaking. Finally he said, "We don't have to do this now, if you want to wait." I finally responded with words, "I want to marry you more that anything in the world. I just have never done something so major without having my parents permission."

We finally arrived at the J.P.'s office. Everything was in order. After a very short ceremony, he pronounced us husband and wife. We did it and my commitment was for life.

4.

THE PLAN

Our plan was that as soon as the school year ended in just a few weeks, that we would sit down again with my parents, but this time it would be to tell them that we were married. We would show them our rings, our marriage license, our budget and share with them our plans to live on our own.

The first morning, I awoke in my bed at home. This was the day that we were planning on telling my parents of our marriage. My mother came into my bedroom and startled me with a question. Not all the way awake yet, I thought I heard her ask me if Jerry and I had gotten married. Oh, no! This was not how we had it planned. Jerry and I were planning on telling my parents that evening together. Not knowing quite how to respond I said, "What makes you think that, Mom?" She said that she happened to find a half written letter to Jerry that said something about us being married. Then before I could say anything, my mother started telling me things that I hadn't considered. She said I was her only daughter and how much it would hurt her if I had gotten married and she hadn't gotten to be there. She went on to say that she had a very small wedding due to lack of money, so she wore a suit instead of a wedding dress. On and on she went about how she was looking forward to planning a big church wedding and helping me pick out the colors, dresses, and flowers. My response was, "Oh no, Mom. We're not married." I immediately felt guilty for lying to my mother, but I didn't want to hurt her. I had no idea how important my wedding was to her.

That evening, instead of Jerry and me telling my parents that we were married, we were once again asking their permission to get married. This time they said, "Yes, but next year." We tried to talk them into having it within the next three months, but the answer stayed the same. Our church wedding was set for June 27, 1964. This would be more than a year from our marriage that had already taken place with a Justice of the Peace. For over a year of actually being married, we were allowed one date a week plus church on Sunday. We would slip on our wedding bands on our date night and immediately remove them at the stroke of twelve midnight, when I had to return home. I didn't go back to campus for my sophomore year, but instead took classes at the extension in Indianapolis, worked a part-time job, and saved money for the time we could openly live together as husband and wife.

5.

MARRIED AGAIN?

*E*leven months after getting married again in a big church wedding, we started our beautiful family – a son named Scott and three years later a daughter named Dawn. Our life revolved around our children. Scott and Jerry shared a love for all sports and Dawn and I shared our love for horses. We also enjoyed family camping vacations. Our family was our life.

Although Jerry was a schoolteacher for the first five years of our marriage, he later took over running our family's wholesale bakery, that my grandfather started in 1929. I was a stay at home mom in those early years.We had what many would consider the ideal family life in our charming home in Carmel. Family and friends were our priorities.

I had attended church as a child and had stated that I believed that Jesus was the Christ, the Son of the Living God. I was baptized at age eleven at North Tacoma Christian Church in Indianapolis, but the Bible seemed like a history book to me. I believed that Jesus was the Son of God the way that I believed that Lincoln had been the President of the United States. It was only head knowledge.

I believed there was a God and so we attended church on Sunday, but it was more of a social gathering to me. When my cousin, Sue, invited me to go to a Bible study, I refused. I stated that the Bible was a history book and was not relevant for today. My cousin was relentless and I finally asked, "If I go one time, will you stop asking me? Her answer was yes, so I went.

6.

BORN AGAIN!

This was not like church although the group met in a church. The first thing that I noticed was the sincere love that everyone had for each other and it was definitely not a "dress up try to impress" group. I really liked that. Then I heard scriptures that suddenly convicted me. (James 2:19 Even demons know that Jesus is the Son of God and they tremble.. I realized that just knowing that Jesus is the Son of God did not make me a Christian. Then I heard (Rev. 3:20 I stand at the door and knock…. I also realized that Christ was knocking on the door of my heart. I had acknowledged Him at the entry but had not invited Him in. (Romans 12:1 Therefore, I urge you brothers, in view of God's mercy, to offer your bodies as living sacrifices, holy and pleasing to God – this is your spiritual act of worship.) I had NOT offered my life to the Lord. I realized that my life had belonged to me and to my family.

I left the Bible study, went home and knelt down in my bathroom. I realized I had been trying to be good and live right so that I might go to Heaven, but now it was clear to me that I couldn't be good enough. No matter how good I tried to be, I was a sinner.

Christ paid the price for my sin. I had acknowledged him as the Son of God, but I had not invited Him into my heart and I had not presented myself to Him as a living sacrifice. I did so that day kneeling by the bathtub.

At the moment that I submitted my life to Christ, Jesus became real to me and I knew that I belonged to Him. I knew that, ("It is not I that lives any longer, but Christ Jesus who lives in me."-Gal.2:20) I went back to the Bible study each week after that with a hunger for God's Word and a desire to grow in the Lord.

7.

POUNDING ON OUR DOOR

*W*e had just celebrated Thanksgiving. Hours after going to bed I heard sounds outside. Someone was knocking on our windows. It sounded like it was coming from our little girl's room. Dawn was just three years old and had gone to sleep hours earlier. I got up to investigate. I walked through the darkness of the house without turning on a light. Suddenly, there was violent pounding on the front door. I ran to our bedroom to get Jerry. Jerry flipped on the lights and opened the front door. A young man with a wild look in his eyes tried to force his way into our house. Jerry grabbed him and threw him out of the door and onto the front lawn. I ran to the phone to call the police, then I returned to the front door. The intruder and Jerry were struggling in our front yard when suddenly the stranger broke loose and came running right for me as I stood just inside the front door.

Just as he reached the door handle, Jerry grabbed him from the back and threw him once again to the ground. As the police arrived and began to put handcuffs on him, the stranger yelled at me. He said, "I'm of a different time and a different place. I will return." His eyes were like beady pin points as he spoke.

The next day I called the police department to ask what happened to this young man. They explained that his wife had just left him. He was on drugs and delusional. They said they thought he was looking for her. I didn't know why he was beating on our windows, nor did I understand why he said such a strange thing directly to me, but I prayed for him. I always remembered those terrifying moments.

8.

TO WHOM DO OUR CHILDREN BELONG?

*O*ur son, Scott, was six years old when he became violently ill. Within just a few hours of showing symptoms, his temperature sky-rocketed to 105 degrees. When I described his symptoms over the phone to the pediatrician, he told us to rush him to the emergency room at Methodist Hospital. As my husband, Jerry, was carrying Scott into the hospital, Scott's eyes were rolling back in his head. He was convulsing. As the hospital staff took Scott away for x-rays, I was reminded of the Bible story of Abraham laying his son Isaac on the altar in obedience to God's direction. Abraham recognized that God had miraculously given him a son and that his son truly belonged to God. Abraham was willing to trust God with his son's life as to whether God would take him back or not. I knew that God was asking me, "Do you trust me with your son?" I knew at that moment my son was not mine, but His. I spoke, "Lord, you alone have created everything there is. You love my son with a love that is deeper than I can even comprehend. I am asking for his healing, but I trust you with the outcome, for you have blessed us with our children, but they truly belong to you."

On Friday, the day we rushed Scott to the hospital, it was determined that he had a very fast acting form of pneumonia. The doctor said that he would probably have to remain in the hospital for at least a week or more as he received the strong antibiotics. During Friday and Saturday, he seemed to be drifting in and out of consciousness. Many people were praying for him. I stayed by his side and slept in a chair in his hospital room. Sunday morning when Scott woke, he seemed alert. He had no fever. The x-ray showed no signs of pneumonia. The doctor came into the room to speak with us. He stated that the antibiotics must have worked very rapidly and that we would be able to take him home. The doctor then put down his paperwork and said, "There is no way of really explaining your little boy's speedy recovery other than it is miraculous." Instead of Scott remaining in the hospital for a week or more, he was able to leave on Sunday, the third day. The doctor was right, it was miraculous. God had answered our prayers for Scott's healing.

9.

FOLLOWING JESUS

I asked the Lord to direct me by giving me an enthusiasm for what He wanted in my life. In 1976 I applied for a teaching position at Heritage Christian School. I was hired to teach 4th grade. Each day our son, Scott, and our daughter, Dawn, and I went to school together. We prayed together and studied His word together. The Lord continued to give me an enthusiasm for His Word and for teaching His Word daily to children at Heritage.

I discovered that the more I submitted my will, my mind, and my heart to the Lord, the more He used me in the lives of others. Reading God's Word regularly, going to Bible studies, and even teaching God's Word are very good activities, but if a person is using it for selfish purposes it can result in a self righteous or holier than thou attitude. All of the good works can result in a type of religiosity. Was that happening to me?

One evening while watching the news on television, I viewed an entire island of massacred men, women, and children. Guerrilla fighters had attacked this island and they had even bayoneted babies. I went to the kitchen with tears streaming down my face. How could anyone do such an evil thing. As I was washing the dishes the Lord spoke to my heart and asked, "What is the worse sin a human can commit ?" In my thoughts I responded, "It's someone who would bayonet a baby." The Lord spoke in my mind as clearly as if in my ears, "It's only through my grace that you have not committed the worst sins imaginable."

At that moment I was overwhelmed with the understanding of my sinful nature and at the same time overjoyed that Christ had died for me for the remission of my sin. With this understanding, how could I ever have a self-righteous attitude. How could I ever point a finger at someone else's sin. (Matthew 7:15 tells us, "Judge not that you be not judged.") We are called to be a light not a judge.

10.

LIFE

*O*ur son, Scott, married his high school sweet-
heart. Within the first six years of their marriage they had three boys - Corey, Joshua, and Luke.
Scott ran the night crew for our family bakery and was
also in the army reserve. He was called to serve during
"Operation Desert Storm." Their marriage ended and
his now former wife remarried. Seven years later,
Scott remarried and had another son named Daniel.
What blessings are our four grandsons!

At age 16, our daughter, Dawn, became a pilot. By
age 19, she had her instrument rating and by 20, her
commercial pilots license. Flying planes and riding
horses were her passions. During Dawn's teenage
years she confided in me that she really didn't think
she would live to be very old. I thought maybe it was
because she did challenging activities like flying and
horseback riding, but I thought that it was strange that

a teenager with a bright future would think that her life would be short when most young people seem to think they are invincible.

In 1986, while still teaching at Heritage, Dawn and I started a summer therapeutic horseback-riding program for children with disabilities. We named the program "Agape" which is a Greek word that refers to God's unconditional love for mankind. Each summer we took our five specially trained horses to Indiana University's Bradford Woods Camp. We worked with over 450 children with disabilities summer after summer. At the end of the summers we had many calls from the parents of the campers telling us how much their child enjoyed the horses and asking us if we would consider having a year-round therapeutic riding program.

That was our dream...to someday have a year-round therapeutic riding program, but that would necessitate having acreage and an indoor riding arena, a financial commitment, and a change in my profession. What if it failed? Fear stood in the way so we did not pursue the vision that God had given us, but we continued to dream about the possibilities.

Time went by. Dawn graduated from college and married a man 17 years older than she, named Bill. They had a son that they called "Little Billy" after his dad. Now we had a fifth grandson. Not long after their child was born, Dawn came to us and told us that her husband, Bill, was very physically abusive. She had hoped after their son was born that he would change, but when the baby would cry, Bill would scream at the infant and shake the crib violently. Dawn realized that the abuse that she was receiving was also going to be inflicted on their child. She knew something had to be done. After they both received counseling, the verbal and physical abuse still continued, so Dawn filed for divorce. In January of 1992, she and her infant son came to our home to live with us. I left my position at Heritage Christian School to be home with Dawn and to give her support.

February was a very special month for Dawn and me. Now that I was home with her everyday, we had time to talk. My once little daughter, now age 23, became my best friend. We shared our deepest feelings, our joys and our sorrows, and our love for the Lord. Dawn expressed her concern for her little baby who was nearing his first birthday. She said that her hope was that their baby would grow up with a loving mom and dad as she had. She asked me the question, " How could her baby ever have a loving home life with an abusive father?" The only answer that I had was that God would provide. We had always been close, but that month we became even closer to each other and closer to our Heavenly Father.

11.

POUNDING ON OUR DOOR, AGAIN

*F*riday morning, February 28, 1992, was different. My husband, Jerry, usually left for work quite early, but that morning he stayed later than normal. Dawn, Jerry, and I sat for over an hour just talking together. Our son, Scott, was already at our family wholesale bakery taking care of running the business.

Shortly after Jerry left for work, there was a pounding at the front door. When Dawn answered the door, there stood her estranged husband, Bill. He burst through the door, knocking Dawn down and demanded, "I want to see my son and I want to see him now!" I ran for the phone to call the police. Bill yelled, "Don't you touch that phone!" I turned toward him just in time to see my son-in-law, who sat next to me in church the previous Sunday, pull something from under his jacket. He pointed a gun at me and pulled the trigger. I felt the stinging of the bullet as it penetrated my abdomen. I felt it exit my back and I found myself on the floor with Bill standing over me. I heard Dawn scream, "You shot my mom!"

12.

IN THE FACE OF DEATH

Bill pointed the gun at my head. I said, "Bill, God loves you and I forgive you." Bill responded, "I don't care about your God; I don't care about your Jesus; I want you to suffer." He fired the gun at my head as I prayed out loud. I felt the bullet graze my head; it stunned me and Bill thought I was dead. My life seemed to flash before my eyes and then I was brought back to the awareness of the moment. Bill had turned his attention toward Dawn. I could hear everything, but I was unable to move. Dawn pleaded, "Please, Bill, I will do anything you say, just let me get help for my mom." I heard a shot, a moan, and then Dawn dropped to the floor. I heard Bill take two steps forward and then another shot as he fired a second bullet into her head.

Bill proceeded upstairs to get "Little Billy" who had been awakened by the gunfire. The baby was screaming as he stood in his crib in the loft bedroom just above his dying mother. Bill grabbed the baby and left. As soon as the door closed behind him, I thought, "Bill is taking the baby. I am not dead and I have to get help." I stood up. Bill saw me through the window. He grabbed the doorknob to get back in, but the door was miraculously locked. He jumped in his car carrying Little Billy and sped away.

I went to the phone to call for help, but the cordless phone was missing. I went to the lower level of our home to call 911, but I couldn't dial out because the missing cordless phone was evidently turned on. I went outside and yelled for help, but no one in our condominiums was home. I began to feel weak as I dropped to my knees and stretched out on the cold hard pavement of the drive. ("Be strong and Courageous. Do not be terrified; Do not be Discouraged, for the Lord your God will be with you where ever you go." Joshua 1:9)

13.

GOD WAS ALWAYS THERE

neighbor decided to come home for lunch that day and happened to see me. He called 911 for help. When the medics arrived they life-lined me to Methodist Hospital. As I was being transported, I asked the Medic how my daughter was. He said that my daughter had died.

I was suddenly filled with an overwhelming peace…a peace that passes all understanding. I knew without a shadow of doubt that Dawn was with the Lord and that I would be with her again for eternity. Instead of crying, I sang a song that begins, "Jesus, Jesus, Jesus, there is something about that name. Master, Savior, Jesus, like the fragrance after the rain." I sang it over and over again until I was transported into the trauma center for emergency surgery.

Bill took Little Billy to his parents' home in Carmel. He went to his truck and when the police arrived he shot himself in the chest. He died before the medics arrived.

Little Billy was removed from Bill's parents home and temporarily placed in foster care. My husband, Jerry, was advised to immediately apply for temporary custody of Little Billy. As soon as Jerry did so, he returned to my bedside in the hospital. My surgery to remove debris left by the bullet as it passed through my liver and nicked my kidney was extensive. I was in and out of consciousness in the hospital for days, but Jerry never left my side. Because of the violent nature of the crime, I was moved to an undisclosed, secured wing of the hospital. During one of my lucid moments, two nurses entered my room. Their words were like sweet healing balm. They said that they knew everything that had happened and said that they would like to pray with us. I don't remember their words, but I do remember their touch. It felt as if we were wrapped in angel wings and lifted up. That's how Jerry describes it, too. We never saw them again.

Dawn's funeral was delayed because I wasn't able to leave the hospital. Our son, Scott, made all of the funeral arrangements and continued running the family baking business. I wasn't able to go to the viewing, but I was taken from the hospital to the funeral and then immediately returned to the hospital.

The church was filled, but I don't remember who was there. Pastor Tommy Paino spoke healing heartfelt words, and Karl Hinkle sang. As he sang, I stood from my wheelchair and raised my hands in praise to my Heavenly Father. I felt my Abba father's loving arms enfold me. God had given us a beautiful daughter for twenty-three years and now He had taken her home with Him. I knew without a shadow of a doubt that I would be with her again for eternity.

14.

LOVE IN ACTION

My physical healing took a while, but now that we had temporary custody of Little Billy, I was eager to take care of him. The problem was that I still was not allowed to lift anything, not even our little grandson. Some dear friends, Dr. Ed and Nancy Fitzgerald, offered to have us stay with them at their home until I was healed enough to care for the baby myself.

The day I was released from the hospital was Little Billy's first birthday. We were at the Fitzgerald's house and we agreed that it would be best to have his name changed, since he had been named after his birth father. His new name was "Michael." This new name was his first birthday gift and a beginning of a new life for him - a life of being raised by a loving mom and dad - a life that Dawn had hoped for her baby.

Jerry and I now made the next step of applying for permanent guardianship. Bill's relatives took us to court to fight for custody themselves. Although Bill's much older parents with failing health didn't want to raise the baby, Bill's youngest sister and her husband did want to raise him. They had three little girls and also wanted a boy. Here was their chance.

Bill had been the oldest of his parent's six children. When they came to the realization of what had happened, all of them began to reflect on their own lives. They all had many questions, so they called one of Bill's former high school friends to ask hard questions about God and His son Jesus Christ. This former friend of Bills ran a Christian tape service, so they felt that maybe he could help answer their questions.

Bill's former friend, Mike, not only answered their questions, but also explained to them how Jesus Christ, the son of God, had lived a perfect life on earth. He represented the unblemished lamb and sin offering, by His death on the cross for our sins. Then by raising from the dead on the third day, He demonstrated His victory over death. Jesus made a way for all mankind to spend eternity with the Heavenly Father. Each person in Bill's family, who had not previously invited Christ into his heart, did so at this time.

(Jesus said, "My command is this: Love each other as I have loved you." John 15:12)

15.

A STRANGE CONNECTION

The court system mandated that Little Billy, who was now Michael to us, would go to his grandparent's house one day each weekend. On one of the visits to Bill's parent's house, I was asked to stay for awhile. One of Bill's brothers got out the high school year book to show me Bill's senior picture. At eighteen, Bill looked nothing like he did as a middle aged man of age 40. Somehow, I knew this eighteen year old face in the yearbook, although I couldn't remember where or how.

A few weeks later, I received a strange telephone call. I was not familiar with the caller's name, but she said something that shocked me. She said that she was Bill's ex-mother-in-law. Since I didn't know that Bill had been married before, I was very surprised. She told me that Bill and her daughter were married right out of high school. Shortly after their marriage, Bill became very abusive to their daughter. He was often high on drugs and his rage was relentless. Their daughter finally came home to live with her parents and filed for divorce. What she told me next sent chills down my spine. She said that Bill would come to their house late in the evening, high on drugs, and beat on their windows and doors trying to find their daughter.

Then I knew why Bill's senior picture looked so familiar to me. Could it be? Was he the young man pounding on our windows and door? The one that Jerry threw out of our house onto the ground? The one who looked at me with the same beady eyes that Bill had when he shot me? The one who said, "I'm of a different time and a different place. I will return?"

Twenty years before when I had called the police to find out about the young man who had tried to get in our house. They had told me that he was on drugs and that his wife was divorcing him. He thought he was at her house and was trying to get to her.

Could that have been Bill, so many years before? While under the influence of drugs, was he influenced by unseen demonic forces? Did his seemingly bazaar statement actually come to fruition?

This seems like a story that we only hear in the news, or science fiction, not something that would happen to us or anyone we would know. I thought again of the verse, "All things work together for good for those who love the Lord.... I was reminded of the story of Joseph in the Bible. Joseph said, "What they meant for evil, God has meant for good." God was already changing something that was meant for evil into something good by bringing Bill's brothers, sisters, and their families into a closer relationship with Christ.

When someone experiences a tragedy in his life, it is difficult to see how good is going to come from it. That's where faith comes in. Trusting God with the out come, believing that God is in control even when everything seems out of control. This is the essence of faith.

16.

COURAGE TO MOVE FORWARD

*D*uring that time when I was recovering in the hospital, my husband and I had prayed, asking the Lord to show us His will and the direction for our lives. We knew first of all that we were to forgive and we knew that as soon as we received permanent guardianship, we were to adopt Bill and Dawn's baby boy. We gave Little Billy a new name on his first birthday. Michael William Miller celebrated his first birthday with his new name on the day I was released from the hospital, but his new name was not yet official.

The first year after Dawn's death carried with it additional struggles because Bill's parents and siblings took us to court as they tried to fight us for the permanent guardianship of Michael. Again the Lord reminded me of his forgiveness and how He wants

His forgiveness and love to flow through us to others even when others are not returning that love. As we showed God's unconditional love to Bill's parents and his three brothers and two sisters, each one appeared to grow in Christ's love. After taking us to court in their efforts to gain custody of the baby, they later thanked us for our love and care of him.

The second thing God impressed upon us was that we were to move ahead with the dream that Dawn and I had of opening a year-round indoor heated riding facility that would help individuals reach their God given potential by using horses as a means of therapy. The Lord gave us peace and showed us clearly the direction that He wanted us to go. As we put Christ first, He strengthened us and we no longer feared moving ahead to make the dream of a year-round therapeutic riding center a reality. We purchased acreage in Cicero, Indiana, built an indoor heated riding arena, and opened the Agape' Therapeutic Riding Center in February 1994, exactly two years after Dawn's death. Agape's mission was to "Glorify Christ by serving others" using horses to benefit individuals with physical, mental, and emotional disabilities and youth at risk. It was truly God's provision for healing us and healing others. ("Forgive as the Lord forgave you" – Col. 3:13b)

17.

FROM PAST TO PRESENT

*A*gape' Therapeutic Riding Resources began its history as a year-round program with only one paid part-time instructor named Chris and three and one-half non-paid employees, our 29 years old son, Scott, my husband, Jerry, 50 years old, baby Michael 3 years old, and myself at 49 years old. We all worked hard doing anything that needed to be done, even though Scott and Jerry were still doing their full time jobs running our family baking business. God provided volunteers and support to help this special non-profit ministry.

We didn't have the time or money to advertise, but people came. Funding began to come into Agape' through grants and donations. People came to Agape through word of mouth. Soon we were able to hire more employees. Horses and tack were donated. Two world renown horse whisperers did fund raising events for us. God was moving in a mighty way and He was transforming lives in miraculous ways.

Tommy, an 11 year old boy with Autism, spoke his first word to his horse. He has been talking ever since. Caleb, at almost three years old, couldn't sit up, couldn't support any weight on his weak legs and didn't understand the concept of chewing solid food. Within six months of therapy on a horse, his balance had improved so much that he was able to sit. His muscle strength had increased so much that he could pull himself up into a standing position and take five steps all by himself. Oh, yes, about the chewing.... although this was not a goal for Caleb at Agape', because Caleb brought an apple for his horse each week and watched the horse chew, his mother said to Caleb, "Chew like the horse." Caleb understood and ate solid food from then on.

Lives were truly transformed as our Heavenly Father touched the lives of so many individuals with His Agape' - Unconditional Love.

Time has passed. Jerry and I have now been married over fifty years. Now Agape' serves thousands of individuals each year. Not only has God provided the year-round Agape' Therapeutic Riding program north of Indianapolis in Cicero, IN, but also south of Indy at Bradford Woods in Martinsville IN, where Dawn and I began the summer therapeutic riding program years ago. Here an indoor riding facility has been built for Agape' to provide their unique programs during all seasons. We not only serve the local individuals at both locations, but also the individuals throughout the state of Indiana. Agape's scope of service includes all ages from very young children to the elderly, from students to veterans, from those with physical, mental, and emotional special needs to those who have been abused, from rehab patients to adoptees. Serving others is serving the Lord and doing it with His Agape' love is powerful and has amazing results.

God has truly turned what was meant for evil into something that is meant for good. He does work all things to together for good for those who love him. ("And we know in all things God works for the good of those who love him..." Romans 8:28)

18.

TRIUMPH

*T*hrough life, I have realized that when we receive Jesus Christ as our Lord and Savior, He not only forgives our sins, but we become new creatures in Christ. We can then say, "It is not I who lives, but Christ Jesus lives in me."

Then how can we not forgive others no matter what they have done to us. We **can** forgive if we allow Christ to reign in our lives.

When Christ reigns miracles happen:

Grief is turned into Rejoicing.

Anger is turned into Understanding.

Hatred is turned into Compassion.

Fear is turned into Courage.

Death is turned into Life.

Tragedy is turned into Triumph.

It is your choice to allow Christ to reign in your life or not.

It is your choice to be bitter or better.

God gives us free will. What will **you** choose?

19.

MIRACLES

An eleven year old boy with Autism speaks his first word on the back of a horse; a nineteen year old college student injured in a fatal car accident believes that she will never walk again until she is transferred to the back of a horse, then she goes from a wheelchair to a walker, a walker to a cain, and a cain to walking independently. These are only two of the many individuals helped through teaming up with a horse to serve the Lord at the Agape Therapeutic Riding Center.

Jesus said, "Very truly I tell you, whoever believes in me will do the works I have been doing, and **they will do even greater things than these,** because I am going to the Father."

What is a miracle? To some it is only a person touched by Christ and his blindness is healed, or a lame man told by Jesus to stand up and walk and he immediately stands and walks. They also believe that these miracles only happened when Jesus Christ walked on the earth. But what did Jesus say?

As a Christ follower, you are the hands and feet of Jesus; collectively we are the body of Christ. Do you truly believe what Jesus says? Philippians 4:13 says "I can do **all things** through Christ who strengthens me."

MIRACLE STORY 1. Caleb came to Agape with his mother when he was almost 3 years old. His balance was so poor that he was unable to sit on the floor and play without falling over. His muscles were so weak that if you tried to stand him up, his little legs would fold beneath him. Caleb did not come to Agape to learn to ride a horse, instead he came for the therapy that he would receive by being placed in specific positions on the horse's warm dynamic back. Caleb's mother also happened to mention that he did not understand the concept of chewing solid food.

Caleb's therapy began in May. Each week he and his mother brought an apple for Duke, the beautiful palomino horse on which he received therapy. Sometimes the therapist would have Caleb sit on the horse facing backward with support while he reached for toys that the therapist would place on the horse's rump. All the while the horse would walk in a steady rhythm around the indoor arena. As Caleb progressed, the therapist would sit on the back of the horse and support Caleb in a standing position with his feet resting on the horse's bare back near the withers. By the end of September of the same year, Caleb's balance had improved so much that he could sit indefinitely on the floor without falling over. His strength had increased so much that he could pull himself up into a standing position and take five steps by himself. Another miracle that took place was in regard to Caleb's understanding of chewing solid food. One day at home, when his mother was again encouraging him to chew his food, she said, "<u>Caleb chew like Duke.</u>" Caleb had watched that beautiful golden horse chew the apple each week and now he understood what his mother meant about chewing his food. Caleb chewed solid food, sat up tall, and walked without assistance from then on.

MIRACLE STORY 2. Rebecca, a very bright ten year old, arrived at Agape in her wheelchair. She was wearing a t-shirt with galloping horses on it, but she was not wearing long pants or closed toed shoes as Agape requires. In fact, Rebecca was wearing no pants or shoes at all, because her legs had been amputated at birth due to extreme malformation caused by spina bifida.

Her first question was, "Do you think that I will be able to ride a horse?" Without a single hesitation I said, "Absolutely." Did I just hear that word come out of my mouth? We had never had a rider with no legs, but yet deep in my heart I knew that she would be able to do it.

After her first ride on an English saddle, with a trained volunteer walking next to the horse on each side of her and a volunteer leading the horse, Rebecca couldn't stop smiling. She then told us that she would like to get on the horse all by herself next time. As I thought about this, I realized that if she could reach from her wheelchair that was positioned on the ramp next to the horse, that she might be able to grab onto the horn of a Western saddle (instead of an English saddle) and swing herself on. That's exactly what she did in her second lesson. From then on, she rode on a Western saddle. Soon she didn't need side walkers on each side of her. As her goals for accomplishments kept growing, so did her skills. Soon she no longer needed a volunteer to lead the horse. Rebecca became an independent rider at a walk, trot, and canter. Wow, what a miracle.

Because Rebecca moved to another state, we didn't hear much about her until her mother called us over ten years later. She wanted us to know that Rebecca had graduated from college and had a very good job. She told everyone that she knew that when she learned to ride a big thousand pound horse all by herself that there wasn't anything that she couldn't accomplish.

MIRACLE STORY 3. The largest school system in Indiana hesitated even considering the possibility of bringing children to Agape during the school day. It appeared to the head of special education that it would not benefit their special needs student much. After we secured a grant for the purpose of providing eight weeks of riding time for special needs school students, the school system agreed to try the program for eight weeks.

The class was selected by the head of special education. The plan was now in place for one class to come to Agape one day a week for an hour and a half each week. The school bus arrived and a class of seventeen children between the ages of six and twelve with severe autism arrived. They entered the observation room and as if a switch had been turned on, all seventeen children began to have meltdowns at one time until the horses were lead into the arena. During their meltdowns students began to notice the horses through the observation windows. As they did, they began to quiet down. One student at a time was assisted onto a horse.

As I helped Tommy onto the horse, I said to him, "Tommy, if you want your horse to go tell him to walk on." Tommy said, "Walk," and his teachers began to cry. I soon found out that Tommy, who was eleven years old, had never spoken a word. His first word was inspired by a horse. After that Tommy began to use other words at school to communicate ideas and requests such as, "Tie shoes."

The school system no longer had any reservations about the benefits of therapeutic horseback riding. From that point on they have sent classes every week to Agape and there have been many more miracles.

MANY MORE MIRACLES HAVE HAPPENED AND MANY MORE TO COME. These have been just a few of the amazing stories of Agape participants. God has used this program and continues to use it to help each person to reach his/her God-given potential. Please call to visit either of our two facilities - Agape North in Cicero, Indiana and Agape South in Martinsville, Indiana.

Call (317) 773-RIDE or go to our website at www. agaperiding.org.

BIBLIOGRAPHY

All Scripture is from the NIV Bible.

CPSIA information can be obtained
at www.ICGtesting.com
Printed in the USA
BVHW09s0733100718
521246BV00007B/105/P